Guide to Profitability

by

Ms. Hetal Shah

Contents

Introduction

Profit is a deeply moral concept, since without profit we will suffer, not from exploitation, but from a misallocation of resources, a failure to provide the goods and services that the economy needs, the nation's loss of tax revenue, a reduction in employment and the inability to provide for social change.

Profit proves that the economy is not a zero-sum game. It is the reward for putting capital at risk. It shows that entrepreneurs are welcome. It generates investment and employment in the world. It provides a means for social transformation.

Some Quotes about Profit:

"Nobody ever lost money taking a profit."
Bernard Baruch

"Running a business well means knowing when it's time to make profit."

"Profit is not something to add on at the end, it is something to plan for in the beginning."

"Where profit is, loss is hidden nearby."
Japanese Proverb

"The successful man will profit from his mistakes and try again in a different way."

"If you keep an eye on the profit, you are going to skimp on the product. But if you focus on making really great products, then the profits will follow." Steve Jobs

"Profit for a company is like oxygen for a person. If you don't have enough of it, you're out of the game. But if you think your life is about breathing, you're really missing something." Peter Drucker

"Form follows profit is the aesthetic principle of our times." Richard Rogers

A Simple Consulting Case Interview

The Profitability Framework is as follows:
Profits = Revenues – Costs
Revenues = Volume * Price/unit
Costs = Fixed Costs + Volume * Cost/unit

Situation:

Your client owns a small independent movie theater in South Carolina. The profits of the theater have gone down during the last 12 months, and the client wants to know why. In addition to providing you with the following tabular data, the client informs you about the real estate rental expansion project to double its capacity.

Cinema	Last year	This year
Profits	$552,000	$404,000
Revenues	$1,400,000	$1,900,000
# of visits	100,000	150,000
$ spent/visit	$14	$13
On ticket	$10	$10
On food/drink	$4	$3
Costs	$848,000	$1,496,000
Fixed Costs		
Rent	$120,000	$240,000

Staff	$288,000	$576,000
Movie Rights	$240,000	$480,000
Variable Costs		
Food Costs	$200,000	$200,000

Consultant Insights:

It looks like revenues have gone up, but profits have gone down, so the issue must be the rise in costs. Upon closer examination, the revenues have not doubled, and have not kept up with the increase in costs. The number of visits has increased by only 50% which could be because of inadequate number of screenings, inadequate advertising, ill-chosen screenings, rise of competitors or substitutes, or unjustified real estate expansion. The average spend on food/drink has decreased by 25%, which could be because the new extension may not have a bar, the food offerings may be ill-chosen, or inadequate advertising.

Conclusion:

The client should make sure that the real estate expansion was justified and nonreversible. Then they should focus on increasing the number of visits to the theater, and the amount customers spend on food/drink per visit.

The Income Statement

Following is a sample Income statement for a successful large corporation in the United States. The dollar amounts are in millions, and the specific year end date is mentioned.

Income Statement	2018
Revenue	
Product	
Service and other	
Total Revenue	
Cost of Revenue	
Product	
Service and other	
Total Cost of Revenue	
Gross Profit	
Research and Development	
Sales and Marketing	
General and Administrative	
Impairment and restructuring	
Operating Income	
Other Income (expense)	
Income before income taxes	
Provision for taxes	
Net Income	

Earnings per Share	
Weighted average shares outstanding	
Cash dividends per share	

The higher the revenues, the higher is the gross profit. The lower the cost of revenue, the higher is the gross profit. The lower the operating expenses, the higher is the operating income. The higher the other income, the higher is the net income. The lower the taxes, the higher is the net income. The lower the number of shares outstanding, the higher are the earnings per share.

You can increase revenue by increasing the revenue per product line, per customer type, per distribution channel, or per geography. Please ensure that the amounts spent on returns, refunds and discounts are reasonable. The goal is to make sales repeatable and scalable. Please ensure that the cost of customer acquisition, customer lifetime value, usage frequency and number of repeat buys are favorable. Please confirm that the churn rates are low, and profitability targets are achievable.

You can decrease the cost of revenue by decreasing the fixed costs such as rent, utilities, equipment, and by decreasing variable costs like raw materials, delivery, commission and payroll. Please note that decreasing fixed costs may compromise the reputation of the company, and decreasing variable costs may compromise the integrity and quality of the products/services sold.

You can decrease the operating expenses by decreasing expenses like salaries, depreciation, advertising, office expenses, repairs, insurance, information technology, travel, subscriptions, utilities, gifts, research and development expenses, sales and marketing expenses, general administrative expenses, and restructuring expenses. Please note that decreasing operating expenses may compromise the integrity and quality of customer operations. Many a times, operating expenses are incurred with the intention of generating revenue, and you need to achieve a fine balance to generate a fine operating income.

Ramifications of a High Operating Income

Profits are necessary for the long-term survival of a corporation. As profit grows, equity grows, and so does vendor/lender debt. Lenders usually don't want to lend money to an unprofitable company. The market value of a company depends on the EBITDA. It is a measure of the effectiveness of the management team. It can be used to pay down debt and build working capital. It attracts investors and better employees. It can be used to pay bonuses and distributions. It increases retained earnings and cash. It can be used to give gifts and donations.

Operating Income is often used to determine if a company is a good investment candidate. Sometimes there is a big difference between a corporation's operating income and its net income. This is due to:

- Non-recurring gains/losses
- Interest paid/received
- Provision for taxes

Examples of Non-recurring gains/losses are:

- Write-offs or Write-downs of inventory or receivables
- Restructuring cost when acquiring & integrating a new company or implementing changes within an existing one
- Gains/losses from sale of assets in subsidiaries/affiliates
- Gains/losses from sale of investments
- Gains/losses incurred from a law suit
- Loss incurred from plant shutdown
- Compensation for expropriation of company property
- Employee separation costs
- Uninsured losses incurred by the company as a result of natural calamities
- Unusual weather related damage to a property
- Damage caused due to fire in plant
- Gain or loss from early retirement of debt
- Gain/loss on life insurance incurred on casualty
- Write-off of intangible assets
- Spinning off of a product line/group

- Change in inventory management principle from LIFO to FIFO
- Change in the depreciation method from Straight line to Sum of digits

The higher the non-recurring gains a company incurs, the higher is the net income. The lower the non-recurring losses a company incurs, the higher is the net income. The higher the interest a company receives, the higher is net income. The lower the interest a company pays, the higher is the net income. The lower the taxes a company pays, the higher is the net income.

Many investment advisors and CPAs can help your company increase interest income and decrease payable taxes, and thereby increase net income and EPS.

Earnings per Share

EPS is calculated by dividing the company's net income by the weighted average of the number of shares outstanding. If there has been a merger or acquisition, incremental adjustments are applied to the numerator.

The relationship between a company's earnings and its stock price can be complicated. High profits don't necessarily mean a high stock price, and big losses don't always lead to a low stock price. Without earnings it is hard for companies to stay in business for long. Two of the major factors that influence stock price are current earnings and the promise of future earnings. One way earnings influence the price of the stock is how well a company performs against expectations. Before most companies report their quarterly financial results, analysts predict the EPS for the quarter based on the company's guidance and other factors. It is a common practice to underestimate EPS; if a company beats the projected earnings, its stock price will usually go up. But if a company fails to reach the projected earnings, its stock price will most likely decline.

P/E ratio is the ratio of share price to net income or earnings. P/E ratios use trailing or forward earnings. The forward P/E ratio is generally more useful because stock markets tend to look ahead. Investors tend to assign higher-than-average P/E multiples to companies with strong growth prospects. However, stocks with high P/E ratios are also susceptible to sharp corrections if they fail to meet earnings expectations.

When a corporation earns income, it has two choices as to what to do with it: it can retain the earnings so that it can invest in its business or it can distribute it as dividends to shareholders. Any **distribution** of cash or property to the owners of a corporation is known as a distribution.

Whether that distribution is taxable depends on whether the distribution is classified as a dividend or a return of capital. A return of paid-in capital is not taxable, since it is not a profit. Dividends are subject to double taxation, in that the corporation must pay a tax on its profits and the shareholders must pay a tax on the dividends received. A dividend is defined as any distribution of cash or property by a corporation to its owners, but only to the extent that it was paid out of earnings and profit. However, if the corporation does not earn a profit for the current year, dividends can still be paid out of the accumulated earnings, even if a corporation has a current deficit.

In order to **list your corporation** on the NYSE or NASDAQ, there are certain minimum pre-tax income, cash flow or revenue requirements. It is not enough to have a lot of shares outstanding and a large market value in order to be a publicly traded company.

Profitability Ratios

Profitability ratios are used not only to evaluate the financial viability of your company, but are essential in comparing it to others in your industry. You can also look for trends in your company by comparing the ratios over a certain number of years.

Gross profit margin ratio = (Gross profit/sales) x 100
Operating Profit Margin = (Operating Income/Sales) x 100
Net Profit Margin Ratio = (Net Income/Sales) x 100

Breakeven Sales = Fixed expenses + variable expenses
Desired Sales = Fixed expenses + Variable expenses + Desired Operating Income

ROI = Net Income/Total Investment
ROE = Net Income/Total Equity
ROA = Net Income/Total Assets

ROI refers to how much money is made from a specific investment. Standard ROI calculations do not account for debt and can give a false impression of business strength. If you find a positive number when looking at ROI, you know the company has a sound return, and that it uses borrowing to expand, rather than using debt to survive. Make sure that the ROI excludes income from capital improvements made with debt.

ROE refers to how much money is made on the basis of total equity. The higher the debt incurred to finance a business, the lower the ROE. Single-digit ROE percentages often signal poor business strength. A fit company will show a rate of 20 percent ROE or more. According to Dun and Bradstreet, a company should have twice as much income as the debt payments cost.

ROA refers to how much money is made from each dollar of assets controlled. It's a useful number for comparing competing companies in the same industry. The number will vary widely across different industries. Companies that require large initial investments will generally have lower return on assets. ROAs over 5% are generally considered good.

These ratios are useful when you compare the figures for the most recent period with results from earlier periods in your company's history. You can set target ratios for the coming quarters, and strive to meet those goals.

You can also compare your company's ratios to those generated by other businesses in your industry. If your company's ratios are worse than those of other companies, this may indicate that your competitors have found ways to operate more efficiently. Find out where the problem lies and fix it. You should aim to be significantly better than your competitors.

How to Increase Profits

If your company has some profitability objectives, you can achieve them in some of the following ways:

- Using key performance indicators (KPIs) to analyze your strengths and weaknesses
- Regularly reviewing the pricing of your products
- Examining the price elasticity of demand for your products and services
- Frequently timing your discounts and promotions
- Hiring great sales people and refining their commission structure
- Focusing your efforts on the most profitable customers
- Providing premium products
- Charging for the extras you provide
- Winning customer loyalty and intimacy

- Increasing the company brand value in the targeted markets
- Licensing some of your intellectual property
- Developing new product lines
- Finding new market segments
- Negotiating better deals with suppliers
- Building and using relationships with strategic and technology partners
- Building and using relationships with channel resellers
- Experimenting with new distribution channels
- Innovating the business model, products, services, and processes
- Analyzing marketing and making it more cost-efficient
- Keeping your product ahead of the competition
- Eliminating product offerings that have low sales and low margins
- Using spare capacity to increase output
- Decreasing inventory

- Assessing your general and administration business costs
- Reviewing your areas of business waste and reducing them
- Maximizing the cost-effectiveness of your fixed assets
- Creating systems, processes and procedures that are not ignored by employees
- Using efficient equipment
- Increasing staff productivity, performance and accountability
- Avoiding unprofitable projects
- Strategizing for continuous improvement

You can set quarterly goals to target some of the tactics mentioned above, and motivate your team towards disciplined execution. You can set scoreboards for lead and lag measures, and metrics you want to follow.

Metrics for Profitability:

- Profit / Sales
- Profit / Customer

- Profit / Employee
- Profit / Customer Visit
- Profit / Tons
- Profit / Revenue
- Profit / R&D Expenses
- Profit / Manufacturing Costs
- Profit / Marketing Expenses
- Profit / Sales Expenses
- Profit / Total Expenses
- Profit / Sales Channel
- Profit / Market Segment
- Profit / Distribution Channel
- Profit / Reseller
- Profit / Salesperson
- Profit / Support Expenses
- Profit / Product
- Profit / Product Group
- Profit / Units Sold
- Profit / Inventory
- Profit / Accounts Receivable
- Profit / Business Unit
- Profit / Fixed Expenses
- Profit / Variable Expenses
- Profit / Project
- Profit / Investment

- Profit / Total Assets
- Profit / Total Equity
- Profit / Shares Outstanding
- Profit / User

Examples of Profitable Companies

Most Profitable Companies in the United States in 2017 according to Fortune.com:

Company	Profits (millions)
Apple	$48,351
Berkshire Hathaway	$44,940
Verizon	$30,101
AT&T	$29,450
JP Morgan Chase	$24,441
Comcast	$22,714
Wells Fargo	$22,183
Pfizer	$21,308
Microsoft	$21,204
Exxon Mobil	$19,710
Bank of America	$18,232
Facebook	$15,934
Procter & Gamble	$15,326
Alphabet	$12,662
Kraft Heinz	$10,999

2018 Profits

According to CNBC.com, Saudi Aramco made a whopping $111 billion in 2018. By comparison, Apple made $59.53 billion in fiscal 2018. Saudi Aramco made more money than J.P. Morgan Chase, Alphabet, Facebook and Exxon Mobil combined. Put together, those companies made nearly $106 billion in 2018, according to FactSet.

Profit Models

According to Thomas H. Byers, Richard C. Dorf and Andrew J. Nelson, there are nine types of profit models:

Name	Description	Examples
Installed Base	Build a large installed base of customers and sell consumables or upgrades	Dropbox HP Printers
Protected Innovation	Create a unique, innovative product and protect it using patents and copyrights	Merck Microsoft
New Business Model	Find unmet customer needs and build a new business model	Twitter Square
Value Chain Specialization	Specialize in one or two functions on a value chain	Nucor Intel
Brand	Create a valued brand for your product	Google Apple
Blockbuster	Focus on creating a series of big winners	Pixar Schering Plough

Profit Multiplier	Build a system that reuses a product in many forms	Samsung Virgin Group
Solution	Shift from product to unique total solutions	General Electric IBM
Low Cost	Create a low-cost product to create a low price per unit of value	Ryanair Airbnb

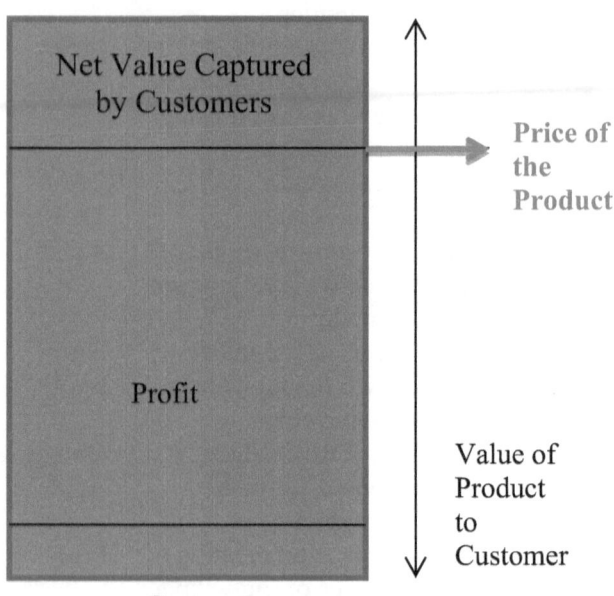

Profit Margins and Volumes

- Low Volume, High Margin   e.g. BMW
- High Volume, Low Margin   e.g. Amazon
- High Volume, High Margin   e.g. Apple

Organic Growth

Organic Growth is growth enabled by internally generated funds. The profitability of a firm is a function of its growth rate of revenues. At a low revenue growth rate, the firm loses sales to its competitors, and at a very high revenue growth rate, it is unable to efficiently manage its operations. The Sustainable Growth Rate is inversely proportional to total assets, and directly proportional to debt and profit. Some companies succeed at maintaining a balance of internally and externally financed revenue growth.

Revenue Growth and Profitability

The following is a list of commonly found **revenue models** in the United States:

- Markup
- Arbitrage
- Licensing
- Commission
- Rent/lease
- Subscription
- Advertising
- Pay-as-you-go
- Interest
- Donation
- Affiliate
- Product is free but pay for service
- Freemium

It is not possible to maximize growth and profitability at the same time. You are either in a rapid growth phase with depressed profits, or you are in a maximizing profit phase with your foot off the growth accelerator.

Steady growth means ensuring that there is no shortage or excess of cash. By discounting future cash flow back to the present day, the current value of the business can be assessed. But sales growth is the prime factor that builds the business's total value. If you want to improve cash flow while the revenues are growing fast, then focus on the customers which provide a better return on investment, and improve the operational efficiency of the company. Please note that unplanned growth can result in major cash deficits.

Balancing revenue growth and profitability

The conventional answer is to seek "balance" between a focused portfolio and a diversified one,
between organic and inorganic growth, and between exposure to high-margin business and high-growth business. The few companies that are able to achieve both profitability and growth at the same time span a range that includes all degrees of portfolio diversity, all levels of acquisitiveness, and all types of industry exposure, balanced or otherwise.

You do not want to increase profits by sacrificing revenue growth, so penny pinching on marketing and sales expenses is not recommended. Often times, revenue growth and profitability can be achieved by doing the following:

- Focus on the customer benefit and improve the quality of the products
- Increase the size of the market instead of just the market share
- Get rid of bad costs, but keep the good costs
- Define which customer segments to focus on, the competitive advantages, and the profitable price points
- Develop unique value propositions for cross-selling to customers
- Focus on the customers that provide a greater return on investment
- Include rewards and penalties for how employees manage the growth budget
- Ensure that the company is innovative and there are daily improvements in activities

- Ensure that employees are aware of the important profit metrics
- Make the company operations cost efficient
- Adopt new revenue models that have greater profitability
- Spend money on sales and marketing expenses befittingly

Market Share and Profitability

Many companies struggle about whether to focus their growth strategy on strong profit margins or increased market share. While ideally businesses would like to have both, they generally tend to favor one over the other. Each has advantages and disadvantages. Strong profit ratios tend to be favored by investors; however, increased market share bodes well for long-term growth.

According to Adrian J. Slywotzky and David J. Morrison, market share used to be the guiding light of the product-centric age. Companies used to strive to grow market share thinking that profits would follow. But there are countless examples of companies with high market share and low profitability and low shareholder value.

According to Rumelt and Wensley, it is necessary to subtract the cost of getting market share from the long-term profits.

The cost of getting market share includes price-cutting, promotions, advertising, R&D, and quality adjustments. These expenses often supersede the long-term profits gained as a result of a higher market share.

According to the Boston Consulting Group, diversified companies often state it as a policy to participate only in those markets where they can occupy the number one or number two spot.

According to Birger Wernerfelt, companies should select the industries they want to be in, and attack in periods of turbulence, such as the early stages of the product life cycle. If a company finds itself in stable asymmetric industry equilibrium, a higher market share will correspond to a higher profit from that time on. Too big a market share may not be optimal for the company. Equilibrium market share is an indicator of the company's relative cost position and the price sensitivity of demand. Now and then, opportunities to switch the relative cost and demand elasticity positions occur later in the product life cycle. Upon executing budgeted tactics for gaining market share, the company can increase its profits.

According to Kevin Laverty, research into the correlation between market share and profitability has led to debate over whether the observed association is direct or spurious. The direct association between market share and profitability depends upon restrictive statistical assumptions. When these assumptions are relaxed, the results show that there is no direct association between market share and profitability.

A higher market share indicates higher sales revenue. A significantly higher market share indicates a higher gross profit. However, two companies with the same market share in the same industry may have significantly different net incomes. All companies are unique. Increasing the market share may increase profitability if rationally budgeted attack tactics are deployed.

About the Author

Ms. Hetal Shah is an expert in strategy, innovation, entrepreneurship and product management. She has over 10 years of professional work experience in the sales, marketing, operations, administrative and entrepreneurial fields. She has worked in the financial services, philanthropy, technology and management consulting sectors. She has worked for four technology startups in the past. She is knowledgeable about the software and telecommunications industries. She was born in 1972. She attained a bachelor's degree in Civil engineering from Bradley University in 1993. In 2001, she was a founder and CEO of a telecommunications-media startup in Boston. Now, she is a business coach and independent management consultant in Boston. She has lived in the Boston area for over 22 years. She is well-read about business, finance and entrepreneurship. She is looking for artificial intelligence, robotics, software and telecommunications companies as clients for her independent management consulting services. She can be reached at hetaliscoy@yahoo.com.

www.ingramcontent.com/pod-product-compliance
Lightning Source LLC
Chambersburg PA
CBHW021851170526
45157CB00006B/2401